The
Imaginative
Explorer's Guide
to the Mall

Eric Braun

SALE
BLACK
RABBIT
BOOKS

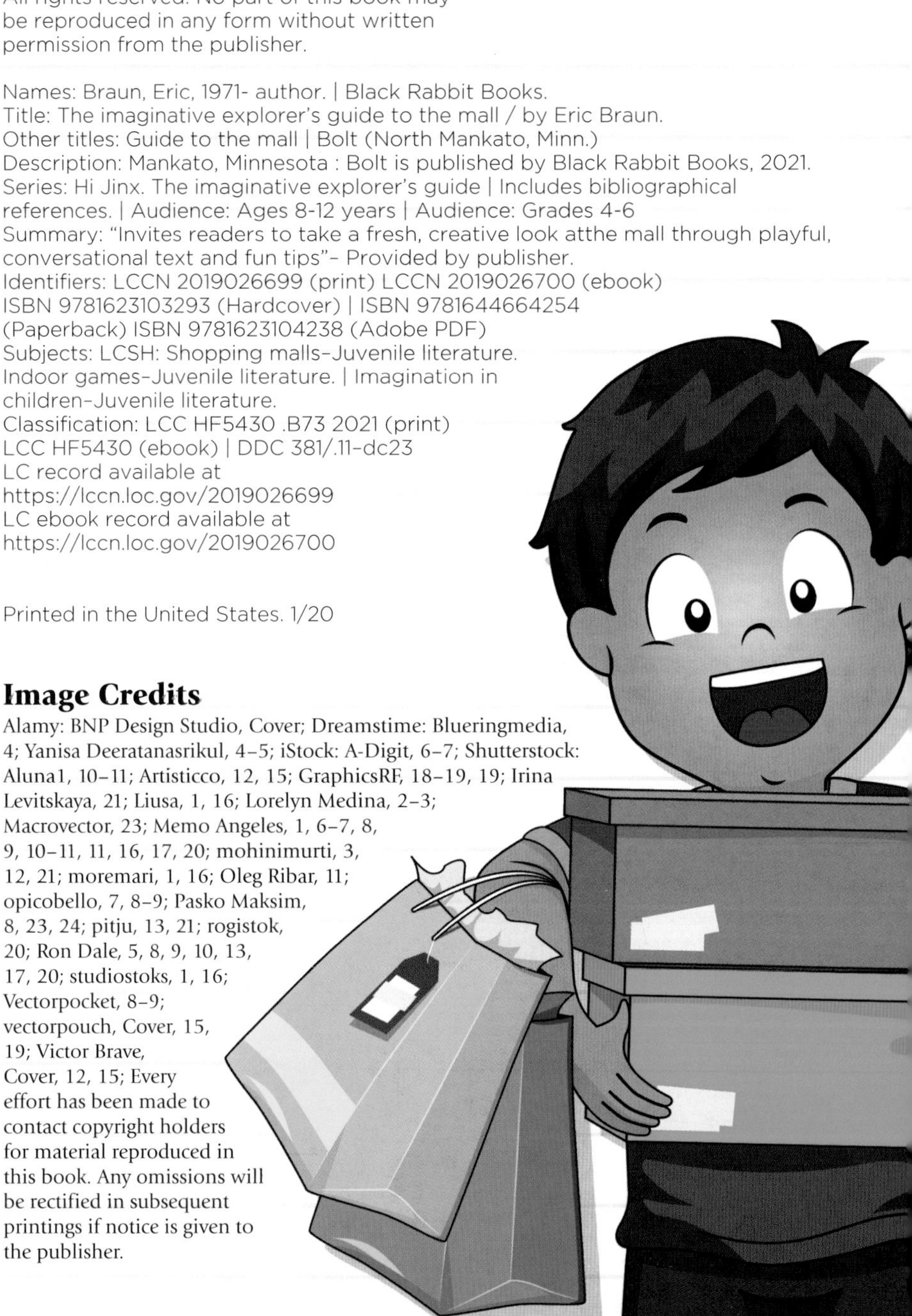

Hi Jinx is published by Black Rabbit Books
P.O. Box 3263, Mankato, Minnesota, 56002.
www.blackrabbitbooks.com

Marysa Storm, editor; Michael Sellner, designer;
Omay Ayres, photo researcher

Names: Braun, Eric, 1971- author. | Black Rabbit Books.
Title: The imaginative explorer's guide to the mall / by Eric Braun.
Other titles: Guide to the mall | Bolt (North Mankato, Minn.)
Description: Mankato, Minnesota : Bolt is published by Black Rabbit Books, 2021.
Series: Hi Jinx. The imaginative explorer's guide | Includes bibliographical
references. | Audience: Ages 8-12 years | Audience: Grades 4-6
Summary: "Invites readers to take a fresh, creative look atthe mall through playful,
conversational text and fun tips"- Provided by publisher.
Identifiers: LCCN 2019026699 (print) LCCN 2019026700 (ebook)
ISBN 9781623103293 (Hardcover) | ISBN 9781644664254
(Paperback) ISBN 9781623104238 (Adobe PDF)
Subjects: LCSH: Shopping malls-Juvenile literature.
Indoor games-Juvenile literature. | Imagination in
children-Juvenile literature.
Classification: LCC HF5430 .B73 2021 (print)
LCC HF5430 (ebook) | DDC 381/.11-dc23
LC record available at
https://lccn.loc.gov/2019026699
LC ebook record available at
https://lccn.loc.gov/2019026700

Printed in the United States. 1/20

Image Credits

Alamy: BNP Design Studio, Cover; Dreamstime: Blueringmedia, 4; Yanisa Deeratanasrikul, 4–5; iStock: A-Digit, 6–7; Shutterstock: Aluna1, 10–11; Artisticco, 12, 15; GraphicsRF, 18–19, 19; Irina Levitskaya, 21; Liusa, 1, 16; Lorelyn Medina, 2–3; Macrovector, 23; Memo Angeles, 1, 6–7, 8, 9, 10–11, 11, 16, 17, 20; mohinimurti, 3, 12, 21; moremari, 1, 16; Oleg Ribar, 11; opicobello, 7, 8–9; Pasko Maksim, 8, 23, 24; pitju, 13, 21; rogistok, 20; Ron Dale, 5, 8, 9, 10, 13, 17, 20; studiostoks, 1, 16; Vectorpocket, 8–9; vectorpouch, Cover, 15, 19; Victor Brave, Cover, 12, 15; Every effort has been made to contact copyright holders for material reproduced in this book. Any omissions will be rectified in subsequent printings if notice is given to the publisher.

Contents

Chapter 1

Spit out Boredom

Good gravy, you're really bored. You've been snacking and snacking just for something to do! You baked cookies. You poured a big **combo**-bowl of cereal. (It had fruity rings, flakes, and granola with taco meat and shredded cheese.) You even ate vegetables! That's how bored you are. You need to bite off something to do. Why not go to the mall?

In the Halls of the Mall

Sure, the mall can get old pretty fast. (Especially if you don't have extra money to spend!) But some imagination is all it takes to turn the mall into a fun new world. Grab your imagination, and get exploring!

Tip
It's fun to people watch at the mall. But it's not polite to stare. Don't point or laugh either.

Tip
Be serious when talking to **mannequins**. It's more fun if you don't crack up.

Chapter 2

Making Friends

You can start your mall adventure by giving shoppers a good laugh. Just use your imagination to talk to some mannequins. Head into a big **department store**. Walk up to a mannequin. Look at it and smile. Act like you're listening. Say, "I'm fine. How are you?" Pretend you can hear the mannequin talking back. Then reply and have a conversation. You could **debate** the ending of the latest superhero movie. Or talk about your favorite waffle toppings.

Blending In

You can take the mannequin joke a step further. Freak people out by becoming one! Go to a different store. Find a display with a mannequin. Then strike a pose next to it. Be super still. Wait for someone to look at you. Give them a wink!

Jewelry
Bags
Coffee

Chapter 3
Save the World

You can be more than a mannequin at the mall. You can become a spy, and protect it. **Slink** into an open area. Put a finger to your ear. Pretend you're listening to a tiny headphone. Intelligence officers at Central Command are telling you about a villain. She's on the loose in the mall! Walk around quickly. Talk into your watch to tell Central Command what you see. Find the villain fast. But don't blow your cover!

Talking in Code

Some of the greatest spies work in teams. Bring a friend to the mall with you. Pretend you're both spies. Work together to take down the villain. To stay undercover, make up a code. Say things that sound like stuff people would normally say at the mall. For example, you could say, "I'm craving pizza." But what you would really mean is, "I think she's in the food court."

FOOD COURT
Fried Chicken
PIZZA & PASTA

SALE

Chapter 4

Random Acts of Kindness

After you've saved the world, you can start handing out compliments. Write nice notes on pieces of paper. They can say things like, "You're amazing." Leave them around the mall for people to find. Your notes will be sure to brighten their day!

Free Compliments

You can also give **personalized** compliments. Go to the food court, and find a table. Set up a sign that says, "FREE COMPLIMENTS." Give people that come up a compliment. It'll make their day! (And it just might make your day too.)

There's so much to do at the mall. You just need some imagination to discover it!

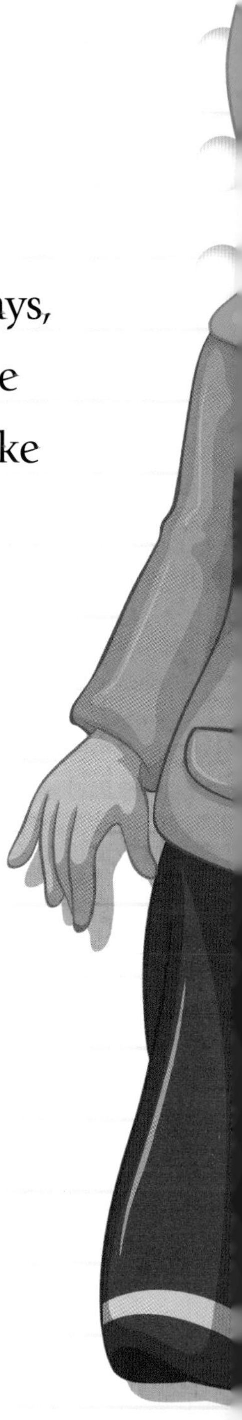

FREE
COMPLIMENTS

Chapter 5

Get in on the Hi Jinx

You can use your imagination to become a spy at the mall. Real-life spies use their imaginations too. They go undercover. While undercover, they pretend they're someone else. Maybe someday, you'll become a real spy. Until then, keep using your imagination to explore the world.

Take It One Step More

1. What is your favorite thing to do at the mall? Why?

2. Do you think malls will be around 20 years from now? Why or why not?

3. Where in the mall could you leave compliments?

GLOSSARY

combo (KOM-boh)—a combination of different things

debate (dih-BEYT)—to discuss something with people whose opinions are different from your own

department store (dih-PAHRT-muhnt STOHR)—a large store that has separate areas in which different kinds of products are sold

mannequin (MAH-ni-kin)—a form representing the human figure, often used to display clothes

personalize (PUR-suh-nl-ahyz)—to mark or change something in a way that shows it belongs to a particular person

slink (SLINGK)—to move in a way that does not attract attention

BOOKS

Caswell, Deanna. *Mastering Spy Techniques.* Spy Kid. Mankato, MN: Black Rabbit Books, 2019.

Devos, Sarah. *I Am Never Bored: The Best Ever Craft and Activity Book for Kids: 100 Great Ideas for Kids to Do When There Is Nothing to Do.* Beverly, MA: Quarry Books, an imprint of The Quarto Group, 2018.

Reeves, Diane Lindsey. *Get a Job at the Shopping Mall.* Get a Job. Ann Arbor, MI: Cherry Lake Publishing, 2017.

WEBSITES

National Geographic Kids
kids.nationalgeographic.com

Spy Facts for Kids
www.dkfindout.com/us/history/spies/

INDEX